My Queer Youth

by Phil Geoffrey Bond

MUFFIN COFFEE

Muffin is the name of our first cat. He's a fully-grown, if not pretty fat creature by the time I meet him when I am born. We live in a charming, two-story suburban home on Banbury Court in Northville, Michigan, a suburb of Detroit, the Birthplace of Soul.

My big brother and I, seven and three respectively, lie on our backs wearing our Osh-Kosh-Be-Gosh play clothes, while Muffin gives us new hairdos with his paws and his tongue. Then, for the next hour or so, we wander about the house and show off our new stylings to whoever will take notice, and remark what a talented and smart cat we have… It's fun.

They say that your drag name is supposed to

be the name of your first pet and your mother's maiden name combined. That would make my drag name Muffin Coffee, which is almost enough to make me want to be a drag queen in and of itself.

THE BOY WHO LOVED BARBRA STREISAND

It's a family gathering, which means one thing: I have an audience. How my five year old self will regale them, dancing to the sounds of The Carpenters atop the wooden floors that adorn the foyay. Actually, the family calls it a foy*er*, but I insist that it 'tis, indeed, a *foyay*. My seven-year-old cousin momentarily tries to share the stage with me, showcasing her mediocre talents, before I dance in front of her, take her by the hand, kiss it, and twirl her behind the stairs.

There is nothing that happens during childhood for which I am more grateful than the taste for good music that is instilled in me. It is my mother who gives me not only the Carpenters, but Aretha Franklin and Anita Baker, Carole King and the glory of Melissa Manchester.

I am seven years old and my mother has come to pick me up from school with the comforting words, "I rented a movie I want you to see." And we drive home to order pizza and to watch the film. And this is among the happiest times of my life. Everything will be fine so long as we have our pizza and our movie. We can leave behind the drudgery, the misery, the nausea-inducing sorrow of our own sorry lives, lives that are so far away from Hollywood or New York, and escape into new, glamorous worlds.

The opening credits begin in a whirl of music and Technicolor. My mother opens the Domino's box and sets two slices, one for each of us, atop her china plates. She sips wine out of one of her fabulous long-stemmed glasses, and she has brought me a glass of milk, knowing how I love the combination of cow and imitation Italian. She sets forks and knives upon the coffee table, and we use folded paper towels for napkins, instead of cloth, and I feel special. It's rare that she allows us to eat anywhere other than a proper table. My mother insists on eating her pizza with a fork and knife, always a lady, and I am proud of this.

I bite into my pizza and this lanky girl in a leopard print coat waltzes across the screen. Shot in Cinemascope, she seems the most vertical person I have ever seen. Those endlessly long fingers and that slanted nose. Then she opens her mouth to sing.

It's slow at first. She makes us both laugh. Then she really starts to sing and I put down my pizza. The Earth has momentarily ceased its rotation and the clouds have parted to make way for a new deity.

There is a familiarity to her voice, like something I once heard in the womb, surrounded by embryonic fluid and oddities. A voice to cry with, and how I will in years to come; a voice like a warm blanket I remember from my infant crib – my stuffed giraffe who protected me through the dangers of a cold night.

Her voice floods the room, the house, the neighborhood, the whole world over. She has reached inside of me and pulled to the surface that which I have always known to be true: *I am the greatest star.* All of the passion and anger and determination that boils within her resides within me also. She knows what I have always known about myself, and she dares to sing it. Too extraordinary to be singing, even, it's just truth, pure – and it emits from every pore of her tiny body. *Try the sky… that'll be me!*

I rush to the record cabinet and I start turning back cover after cover - this chameleon-esque woman, superpower, put on this earth to save us all. And she takes on so many different forms… and hair colors. The women I see staring back at me from the cover of *My Name is Barbra Two* couldn't possibly be the same woman on the cover of *Wet*. My mother mentions something about the consistency of her odd nose, but there doesn't seem to be anything odd about her nose to me at all, it's completely natural, distinct, fitting for a woman who is surely immortal and of another world.

Today I begin an important love affair that will last throughout my entire life. Oh Barbra, how I will massacre your songs in years to come as I belt them out over broken-hearted evenings, alone in my bedroom. How I will pretend I am you as I walk into frightening social situations and confront scary people. How you will bring out the best I have to offer if only by example and inspiration. Barbra… *can you hear me?*

THE MANSION AND THE CONCERT OF MY CAREER

I am nine now, and I am gazing at the back of our new three-story country château in woebegone Columbus, Indiana to whence we have moved. Actually, the family proclaims that it is merely a "house," but I protest, insisting it 'tis, indeed, a *château.* I sit in the middle of a lake from whence I paddle our blue canoe. My dog, Nick Arnstein, looks over the side; his paws perched on the edge of the boat, watching his own reflection ripple in the water.

For small and unassuming little me, our beautiful lakefront residence is the most elegant of mansions, and I the reclusive star who shrouds herself behind drawn curtains. Whenever a car drives past the front, I am certain it is a tourist who has obtained a copy of the map of the movie star's homes. Whenever it's a bus, I know that it is the tourists on a tour of the homes of the rich and famous, or the paparazzi come to snap my photo as I do mundane things like plant my garden or sunbathe in the nude. I am highly suspicious of all helicopters.

I elegantly descend the stone steps in the backyard of my palatial estate, wearing my mother's black patent leather boots that reach up to my knees, the ones with the two inch heel that make me feel like Princess Leia. There is an imaginary audience gathered upon the lawn, and I hear the applause seeping through my headphones that blare Barbra Streisand's *One Voice* cassette, the one I had begged my mother for that very afternoon at Target. The sun is just going down over the lake and I can see the stage lights and feel the dry ice. I lip-sync all of the lyrics to *Somewhere,* as, in my fabulous black boots, I stride all around the backyard, which has transformed itself into my make-shift stage. I am just like Barbra, descending the stone steps in the backyard of my mansion, to which I have invited several hundred of my most intimate acquaintances, to watch me give the concert of my career, ... for *charity,* of course.

ROLLING DOWN THE DRIVEWAY

My big brother has locked me in a closet off the library. The library is really a long hallway in which we've placed some books upon K-mart bought shelves, but I prefer to refer to it as *the library.* Later, after seeing Madeline Kahn in *Clue, the Movie,* I would come to call it "the study."

"You will like rock music," he implores, more of a commandment, a Van Halen-loving hypnotist. My brother's musical tastes stem toward the "hair bands," as they would come to be known. Groups of four or more, dressed in clothes with holes in them, who prove their masculinity by donning hair that reaches down to their waists and is frequently permed, set and colored. And they are called the most attractive names - Def Leopard. Ratt. Poison. Iron Maiden. Anthrax. Megadeath. Twisted Sister (they actually wear eye shadow).

He plops down his enormous silver "ghetto blaster" we used to call them: large silver radio/cassette contraptions with enormous speakers on either end that can literally be seen vibrating when the music is turned up loudly enough, which it frequently is.

"You will like HEAVY METAL, and you will not leave this closet until you do!" He turns up the bass on his enormous shiny bit of technology, leaving his noisy RCA contraption just outside the bars of my prison, and locks me in the closet, knowing full well that mom is not at home and Dad probably never will be again.

I stay in that closet for what seems like many hours, and I hear many things. It's a sweet gesture my brother is making, I realize. He is concerned that his little brother is growing up all wrong, with an attraction to things that stray from the norm, and it is important to him that I learn to try to fit in with mass culture. He is looking out for me, something few people have done, ever. And I recognize the irony in that some people can only appreciate gestures such as these once they've separated them by ten or fifteen years and several hundred miles. But I realize here and now what he's up to. It's kindness, disguised as meanness. And annoying as it is, and loud as it is, it's also flattering. Something about a bitch and her red car and gunshots.

I make my escape when he foolishly turns his

back and leaves the room to smoke a cigarette and to make a phone call to one of his "buds." I dash through the secret annex of our château, down the servants stairs and around through the kitchens, where my imaginary cook, Annabelle, is preparing the evening's meal.

I bolt for the driveway, where I amuse myself sitting atop my skateboard and rolling down the steep slope of our drive, the one that leads to our estate at the top of the hill. I roll down the black asphalt on my skateboard, not standing, but sitting, knees at my chin. At the bottom of the drive, I glide across the street, which is really a *moat* with piranha and alligators, I've decided, and into the grassy median which acts as my break, sending me lunging forward and grass staining my mother selected wardrobe, usually consisting of Izod shorts and shirts of mute colors. Long, white tube socks, the kind with the bands of color at the top, reach almost to each knee. I do not mind getting dirty, and it does not occur to me that things will change, and that one day I will. One day I will come to loathe dirt underneath my fingernails and hair that is askew with the wants of the wind. We think that nature, or whatever the passage of time is, is all well and good for now until one day, we look at our watch, and we can't remember what we were before we learned the rules.

Soon, my big brother discovers the place to whence I have fled. Although he has indeed brought his enormous battery-powered contraption that blares loud obscenities out to the drive with him, having discovered the place to whence I have fled, he's lost interest in forcing me to come around to his liking, and for this I am grateful. He plays an awful cassette until it runs out, something about a substitute teacher and her tight black mini skirt and the misuse of a slide rule, and then it's just the two of us, and the sound of the wheels on the asphalt as we roll down that black driveway and into the grass; first me and then him.

I still don't have a taste for his music; it's true. But then, it's part of him, for whatever reason, isn't it? So it couldn't be all bad. My brother doesn't have much of a taste for Barbra Streisand records, either. But we both continue to roll.

DEAR CAROL BURNETT

Dear Carol Burnett,

Thank you for the autographed photograph and the very nice note. I am pleased to inform you that, over the past six months, I have learned how to type – *entirely as a result of writing you letters.* I'm glad that I know how to type now; it's really come in handy. I like the feel of the keys.

Yesterday, I printed all of the letters I've sent to you ever, and it turned out to be over two hundred pages. Single-spaced. I have read your autobiography, *One More Time*, five times now, which is ironic. I think my letters to you might make for an interesting book if I could find a suitable publisher. Do you know anyone? We could call it *Letters to Carol* maybe? You could write the introduction.

I was pleased to celebrate your birthday last April 26 with a big cake and sparklers, which I lit out on the patio as I sang Happy Birthday to you. Did you know that your birthday is just two days after Barbra Streisand's? Do you know Barbra Streisand? Because, if I come to Hollywood, which I'm planning to, perhaps you could introduce us at some party or show or…

My mean stepfather asked me to say the prayer at dinner last night. The evening prayers usually consist of silly rhythms that don't really mean anything, really, just something ridiculous about meat and drink and Jesus' name. But I said a prayer for you. "God bless Carol Burnett," I said right out loud. I hope you like the flowers I sent, and that they arrived on time. It's your birthday! You only turn --- the age that you are --- once in a lifetime!

I enjoyed watching the show last night on Superstation TBS. You know they do back to back episodes, right? I particularly liked the segments with Charo. I'd like it if you could maybe have Charo on as a guest more frequently? Also, I would like to be on your show. Please write back and let me know when this would be possible. I'll be happy to audition, but I assure you that I'm very good and quite funny. I could come out there, or if you happen to be in Indiana sometime in the near future, perhaps you could come see me play the Cowardly Lion at the Indiana Little Theatre.

Until then, thank you for making the world a

better place, particularly between 6 and 7pm while dinner is cooking… *Thank you.*

Your Friend –

THE LIBRARY

The music that I do like is of silent embarrassment to my family, or rather, *those with whom I live,* as I have chosen to refer to them this year. I am thirteen now, and I've suffered. I'm in the record section of the public library of my small midwestern town. Armed with library card in hand, I take a deep breath and I head over to the forbidden bin marked "Films slash Shows." It's nirvana.

I excitedly start turning back covers like a child who has been given all of his Christmas gifts at once, each demanding to be explored and appreciated. I spend a good hour standing at the bin, looking at all the covers and reading the liner notes. Some of them even have photographs from the original Broadway productions. In later life, I would come to refer to these as *production shots.* Still, I am always careful to look behind my shoulder to see who might be watching me, that weird boy who lives in the big white house atop the hill, flipping through *showtunes* at the public library.

I narrow it down to three records that I will take home with me on this warm summer afternoon: *Funny Girl, Fiddler on the Roof* and *Once Upon a Mattress.* I am completely enamored of both Barbra Streisand and Carol Burnett, and I think that whoever Zero Mostel is might make me look butch to the librarian.

Pensively, embarrassed by my selections and trembling, I walk up to the large oak desk and present my three records, the covers of which I have pressed resiliently against my purple Ocean

Pacific T-shirt, so nobody can see.

The librarian is otherwise occupied. When he finally does come upon me, this *male librarian*, the significance of which totally escapes me, I am trembling in my navy shorts and tube socks (the kind with the bands of color.) He snatches up the records and demands my library card. His face scowls at me underneath over-gelled hair and from behind tiny spectacles, which I suspect are really fashion glasses, meaning the lenses consist merely of ineffective pieces of plastic that serve merely for the *look,* devoid completely of optometry. His yellow, pressed, striped, Liz Claiborne shirt blares out at me, not quite concealing the beaded choker necklace wrapped about his throat. He peers straight into my corneas, and we exchange a kind of known familiarity, and he looks *afraid.* Somebody afraid of *me*... imagine that.

"Can I have somebody else return these,

please, because *they're not for me."* I manage to get this out, quivering more with each word. I cannot allow the librarian to know about my secret dreams of the divas and performing on Broadway in a musical written just for me. I fear he will suspect my tromps through the living room with the blanket wrapped about my shoulders, which I wear as though it were a long, flowing Bob Mackie gown, while I lip-sync all the words to my mother's Melissa Manchester albums.

"I don't care who they're *for*. Why would I care who they're *for?"* Queen Amarantha swipes my card and shoves me away from the desk as quickly as he can. And with that, still shaking and more than a little terrified that he has not presented me with a brown paper bag in which to conceal these embarrassing discs of celluloid which have the power to brand me to anyone who might venture near, I escape the library, and I venture out into the bright Hoosier sun that accompanies a warm day in June. The same sun that makes the corn grow also sheds light on little queer boys and their Barbra Streisand records.

The mean boys who sit upon their skateboards, near the lamppost, glare at me as I walk past. Mean, evil, nasty stares, as though I had just killed Bon Jovi. However, for a change, they say nothing. They just allow me passage, let me *walk on Bi-iiii,* as Dionne Warwick would say, with my records, satisfied with my obedience as I do not make eye contact with them, - segregated. Strangely, almost mystically, they peacefully let me pass without saying so much as a single word, which is most unusual behavior for them.

How did this happen? It must be *the power of Barbra Streisand* which I now posses. Barbra has saved me yet again. These records of hers, clutched between my sweaty hand and my heart which rages with such forbidden intensity. I have triumphed past the lamppost and therefore there is nothing that I cannot do, the sun is, indeed, a ball of butter. I am excited about my new life, free from the oppression of the evil skateboarders, but I am even more excited that in about ten minutes, I will be at home with Barbra and Carol. Turns out that *Fiddler on the Roof* wasn't so bad either.

ALONE IN THE WOODS

"The tracks" is this collection of dirt trails shrouded in the woods, out near the undeveloped part of town. We can easily ride our bikes out there along the sidewalks which belong to pretty subdivisions, which run beside grassy medians and well-furnished homes. Then, we take the dirt trail that leads out to the forest. It isn't too far back; they're not the deepest of woods, but far enough in to elicit at least the tiniest hint of unsupervised danger. Once inside these secret woods, there are ramps and bridges, banked turns and little hills, all sculpted from dirt. It's a hidden fortress of sorts, visible only to youth.

The tracks provide endless hours of entertainment. The big kids pretend they're in a scene from *The Outsiders*, cast far away from parents and suburban rules, a dangerous world consisting of switchblades that double as combs and black leather jackets with excessive zippers. I amuse myself making believe I am Bernadette Peters in a Stephen Sondheim musical.

Our young lives at this age revolve around our bicycles, so the tracks prove to be of great solace. We can hear the traffic on the other side of the thin layer of trees, but we ignore it. We are in a world of our own creation, cast far away from the everyday world of banks and church and grocery stores, experiencing adventures that our young minds will no longer be able to conjure in just a few short years.

I am thrilled when my big brother asks me if I would like to accompany him and his friend, Andrew, out to the tracks. It is a glorious Saturday afternoon in high summer and the trees are swaying beneath an enormous blue sky, lightly scratched with wisps of cloud. My big brother never invites me anywhere, I'm like a bad accessory on an otherwise glamorous outfit, a neon headband worn with a Scazzi gown, an analogy I actually used on him once but which was met with a confused stare. If ever I do venture out to the tracks, it is usually by myself, armed with my Walkman and a Barbra cassette, usually "Stoney End" for situations such as these.

But today is different and, although I will have to take time away from lounging on the sea shore in the south of France with my dog, Nicky

Arnstein, and although I will have to inform the evening maid (Maria), that dinner will have to be late this evening, I mount my red two-wheeler and I head for the woods, pedaling alongside these two Gods of cool.

We pass all of the pretty houses and reach the dirt path. They are strangely quiet. I can tell they are exchanging looks between them as they ride side by side, leaving me behind, my short thirteen-year-old legs pedaling as fast as they can to keep up. Once inside our secret fortress, we make it around the bumpy course once or twice, them flying over the ramps and sailing around the curves on their bikes; me, pedaling leisurely and making believe I can fly and have secret magical powers like I had seen in *E.T.*

Soon, we all sit at the beginning of the course once more, atop our respective vehicles, experiencing a few moments of awkward silence surrounded by the silent trees, who look on with their swooping branches but say nothing.

Andrew looks at me: "I'll take my pants off, if you want." An odd thing to say. However, now that the idea is presented to me… There is a certain curiosity, perhaps even – attraction? – at the notion of seeing what is housed behind Andrew's Levi's. He is big for his age, he has grown quickly; he's everything heterosexual little boys of the 50's loved about Annette on *The Mickey Mouse Club*, only he is a boy, and I find his body *quite alluring*. I guess I always have, really. It does not occur to me that this is wrong. He is beautiful. The same way so many things are beautiful.

"Okay… sure." I am excited and eager. There is something so wonderfully secretive about the woods, something that radiates sexuality where forbidden things might be made possible. I cannot figure why he would want to do it, but my curiosity on this subject does *not* stand in my way: *I want him to.*

He is standing about fifteen feet away with his back to me. He unbuckles his leather belt, unzips his zipper and pulls his jeans to his ankles… he is wearing nothing underneath. He is exposed right there in the shadow of the trees. I stand alone on the other side of the open dirt space, and I gaze upon the two mounds of smooth golden flesh. I think they are very beautiful, and I enjoy looking at them, at what our clothing dictates we are not to see. I have not seen the backsides of many people – only myself, really, if I configure the mirrors in the bathroom appropriately… I want to touch him.

He quickly pulls his jeans back up. "So. What did you think?" My big brother stands, smirking beside him.   "Wow."   I   am   otherwise speechless.

"Wanna see it again?"

"Yes please… That thing was… Wow." As Andrew was several years my senior, perhaps this was the beginning of what would become a lifelong habit of dating older men.

"Just stand over there! We have to talk a second!" I have been banished, cast away from them. My big brother and Andrew conference for several minutes with their backs to me. I hear only strange murmurs and a few chuckles as I gaze at Andrew, down over his backside now covered in faded and well-worn denim. I stand alone, feeling robbed of my second look, waiting, I suppose, for my fate to be decided by a judge and jury of my brother and his friend who has always been mean to me. *Until today,* that is. Maybe he loves me. Finally, they turn around and my brother speaks.

"Well, we've been testing you, and we've decided," he declares, as though issuing a proclamation.

"You're a homo." The words linger on Andrew's lips like poison. They giggle, they laugh. They get on their bikes and speed out of the woods, knowing full well that my young legs are incapable of keeping up even if I wanted to follow them, which I do, very badly. I need to explain to them, I need to apologize, say I hadn't enjoyed it I guess, *something...*

"Homo." This is the first time I have heard the word. I don't even know what it means, but it must be something very bad; a word so bad that it leaves little boys sad.

But too late. I am alone in the woods. And I am scared.

LOVE AT WENDY'S SUPERBAR

That Spring, all of the love songs make sense. What I once didn't understand in Barbra Streisand lyrics, the empty words that I would sing along with but not think too much about, clarify that season. I now know what "soft as an easy chair" *means*... Duh.

My listening repertoire is inundated, consumed with lengthy love songs that go on about doves and trees and waves. I know that I want to be in love very badly, because the songs tell me about how wonderful it is. But I haven't the slightest idea, really, what love *is*.

The tall husky red head is sitting alone in the cafeteria again, the beautiful saxophonist from the school band. He is an outcast, like me. He is unaware of the combined hours I have spent watching him eat his nachos from across the way. He's always reading from *Science as a Tool*, the same textbook I used when I was a sophomore. I am a junior now, fully prepared to offer my tutorial services.

He loves to wear shorts, even in November.

Perhaps it's his silent protest, his refusal to allow summer to die. The red fuzz on his thick legs make them glow, glisten when the sun catches them correctly. The same legs that, when he stands, propel him far from the Earth. He walks through the room with such a commanding presence even though his eyes are downcast. I am astonished that I seem to be the only one taking notice.

His lesbian sister and I are friends. She doesn't know she's a lesbian yet, *but I do.* When we are alone at her house, I ask to see his bedroom. I amuse myself looking over his things and fondling the saxophone that gleams in the corner. I wonder when he will be home and hope it will be soon.

I am sitting on my bed on a pensive Thursday afternoon. School has only been out for an hour. I'm due back for *My Fair Lady* rehearsal at seven, for which I have sharpened my British accent so that I might portray a brilliant if somewhat unconventional Henry Higgins, my favorite thing about the role being that I get to wear an *ascot*.

I stare at the phone. I am about to do the thing I have contemplated for months. Although he and I have only ever spoken a few words to each other in our whole lives, although he is a boy and I am a boy, and although we live in farmland, Indiana; I am going to pick up my Mickey Mouse phone and I am going to ask him out on a date. Tonight.

Come on: I've seen people do it on TV. The world is strewn with couples, people asking each other out right and left, this shouldn't be so terribly difficult. But of course it is.

Enough. I want this - and I'm going to get it. I pick up the phone and I dial the numbers I know so well. My heart is thumping and I feel nauseous as it rings, and rings... and rings. A bit of relief surges through me: nobody's home. I tried and it was a good first attempt. Moving on.

"Hello?" The sister has answered, my friend, the lesbian. Good Lord. I hadn't thought of that. I'll just disguise my voice. No, she won't buy that. I'll just, auh… "Hell – looough?" she persists, as lesbians do.

"Hi, is your brother home?" She's confused, but goes to get him, screaming through the house for all to hear that it is I on the phone and I wish to speak with her *brother*.

"Well, hello there." Now the *mother* has picked up. Ever since my extreme youth, I have been a favorite of the mothers of all of my female friends. I am always the favorite prom date with the mothers. I wonder if the mother will be as thrilled with me if I end up spending as much time with her *son,* as I certainly hope that I might.

"Hello?" It's a deep, strong voice that suits his body. Yet, his voice is innocent, quiet, timid, the sound of wide-eyed perfection.

I have envisioned our affair together, and it flashes across my mind as I try to find the courage to speak into the receiver. How we will carry on an illicit sexual relationship for months, then slowly let the rest of Columbus East High School know about our passion for each other. We will be the first gay couple to be publicly accepted by our small midwestern farming community. *We will be gay heroes.* We will single-handedly change the world. We'll march together in the Columbus Day parade – town celebrities! And people will cheer! How dashing we will look: the red of his hair setting off the black of mine. He is taller than I, he will look debonair standing behind me in our portrait, which we will autograph and hand out in miniature wallet size to all of our friends and fans.

"I saw you eating your nachos in the cafeteria today... They looked especially *crunchy*."

The longest, most uncomfortable silence of my life follows. Okay, enough small talk. Move on. *Jesus.* Maybe he's just being silent in that strong, leading man kind of way.

"Listen, I was just wondering: I have to go and grab some dinner before rehearsal tonight, because I usually eat dinner at nighttime, and since you're in the band and I'm in the play and, I hate to eat alone, I mean, unless I'm rehearsing a monologue or something, - I wondered if you'd *maybe like to come and get something to eat with me?"*

Oh shit. I did it: long, loooong silence. I hate to eat alone? What kind of stupid 40's movie reference was that? More silence. I could have learned the entire Act Three soliloquy from *Henry V* in that silence. Oh, fuck: my stupid life is over.

"What time?"

What was this? The shock feels tangible as it

courses through my bloodstream. "Around five-thirty, okay? I'll pick you up?"

"Sure. See you then. Bye." He hangs up.

I CHARGE into the shower, scrubbing myself clean. I must look my best, but not like I'm placing too much importance on this. Casual. Mustn't scare the boy. I must go to great extremes so that I might look casually thrown together.

Nothing from the International Male catalogue will do. It's all too… too... much. I can't very well show up wearing a pirate shirt or an opera coat. But then, nothing from The Gap seems to really be right, either. *WHAT will I wear??!*

What just happened here? Did I just ask a boy out on a date and did he say yes? Yes. How simple was that? I'm beside myself with shock.

I am terrified driving over in my little blue Honda, my hair itchy from my mother's White Rain hairspray. My nipples scratch against the blue cotton shirt my mother had bought me for church, which we never really attend.

I cannot believe he has said yes. He must be interested. He must share the same feelings as I, he must also envision our future together which, heretofore, I thought only I had foreseen. I am momentarily proud of myself for having the courage to break the silence that the corn instigates.

On the way over to his house, I wish I could stop and pick up some flowers or something for my date. It would make me happy to give them to him. But no, no… don't be too scary.

I have selected all of the correct music; the tapes are lined up in the plastic cup holder beneath the car's cassette player. Kenny G when I pick him up, that will be the first thing he hears upon entering my car. It seems appropriate and quite casual. Then later, after we've broken the ice, I will switch cassettes and put on Barbra as we drive from the restaurant to the theatre for rehearsal. Barbra beat out selections from *West Side Story* or, indeed, Jennifer Holliday's *And I'm Tellin' You I'm Not Goin'*.

Their driveway is curved and long. I step on the gas. I cannot wait. Full speed ahead and then... I arrive.

The whole family is there to greet me. I cannot tell, but it looks to me as though they may be smirking. Out of politeness, I ask the lesbian sister if she'd like to come along, and thank God she says no.

He gets into my car, his manly weight causing the vehicle to slant a little to one side. He's wearing shorts, of course, his trademark; his beautiful bare legs are curled up in the front seat. I drive back down the long drive and I pull out into the street: *we're off!*

He's not talking. I have him for a whole hour

and a half and he is *not* talking. Kenny G wails on his electrified clarinet.

"Where would you like to go?" I had envisioned some quaint little bistro with red wine and tablecloths and an accordion player. Some place with lots of candles and flowers.

"I really love Wendy's super bar."

Assuming he's kidding, I laugh out loud. Then, the reality hits me. Oh, what cruel tricks the fates practice. Although I would rather eat live cockroaches, which if we go to Wendy's, I concede, we just might, I surrender. To Wendy's it is.

We are given our paper cups and plastic containers and, when we reach the cash register with the automatic change drop, I insist on paying with the lunch money I have saved. He does not contest, but looks me in the eye, his deep blue met with my longing green, and he smiles a little. … *He smiles a little.* -- I am *Superman.*

We eat fries and Frosties atop a fiberglass table coated with plastic, old-fashioned newspaper print. We talk of movies and people in school and why he always eats alone. I dare to tell him how I've watched him in the cafeteria. He tells me about his friends in the band and how he's not planning to go to college. He is even more beautiful up close. He smells like soap. Every now and then, he looks up from his burrito and smiles a little, looking me in the eye. He even laughs a few times. I know he likes me. God knows I like him. People glance at us. I am proud of my beautiful date.

Soon we're finished eating and we're walking back to the car. I had hoped that we would fall in love over this dinner, but I don't know how to make that happen – particularly at Wendy's super bar.

Maybe we did just fall in love. Maybe it's

just that subtle.

I start the car and Barbra begins to sing. It is a slow love song, the one I have preselected for this very moment, the one from the end of *The Prince of Tides,* the movie that had come out that year which I saw again and again and again. I ask him what he thinks of Barbra.

"She's okay." Excellent. I can work with this.

His bare, naked, exposed legs stare up at me in the passenger seat: thick and welcoming and beautiful, moving with every pothole. I contemplate reaching out and laying my hand on one of them as I make a deliberately broad gesture while exaggerating some point about how much I like that band he's in, and how great the saxophone parts sound in *My Fair Lady*, of which there are none. We're both due at rehearsal in twenty minutes, we're five minutes from school, and we're stopped at a traffic light. "We're early."

I drive very slowly back to school, well under the speed limit. I don't want this to end. I pray that the music will ignite a fire to match his hair, that the power of Barbra Streisand will surely overcome him and, devoid of his senses, he will kiss me. But it is clear that I am driving in every sense of the word.

He is very quiet now, as though realizing that this is indeed a *date* we have been on, nothing else, and I, like him, am a boy. Do the pieces in his mind form the gorgeous mosaic they do in mine? Could they?

We arrive at school early. A few stragglers loiter in the parking lot. He is quick with his request. "Just drive me around back, by the dumpsters? I can just jump out."

But I know the truth. He cannot be seen getting out of my little blue Honda. He barely says goodbye as I watch him walk briskly into the building, between the dumpsters. He does not look back.

I park. I sit in the parking lot for a long while, listening to Barbra, a rush of embarrassment consuming me. We just couldn't walk in together, could we? We just couldn't.

Once I see that a few of my cast mates have arrived, I venture inside - cautiously. He's climbing up a ladder into the lighting booth when I enter, and I steal a glance up his t-shirt. How I'd like to follow him, spend the rehearsal tucked away in the darkness of that tiny room above the stage. Oh, the things we could do up there, him and me, whilst the rest of the world below remains ignorant. But of course, I stay right where I am, onstage, in a blaring white light; and he ignores me.

School the next day. A few comments about red headed boys are tossed my way. He is not sitting alone in the cafeteria that day, he's nowhere to be found. I miss watching him. Something just happened. Something is very different.

I see him at the end of the day, quite by accident. He avoids my glance, pretending I am not there. He gets up to leave and I watch him walk away. And not one word is uttered.

Dreams that shatter can never really be reborn. They just lie around in pieces for a while until there's no reason to keep them around anymore; and we sweep them up and we toss them out. You smile through the embarrassment, and you start anew some other day.

But he did say *yes*. He did smile and laugh and look into my eyes. He did enjoy himself, he must have; he let me know it in between gulps of Frosty. He even admitted to liking Barbra *just a little*. He did offer me a little glimpse into his world.   He said yes.

KYLE

"If there's a heaven, hon, it's backstage at the theatre," Kyle is always fond of saying. Maybe he didn't mean *community* theatre... but close enough. We are both prominent members of the Indiana Little Theatre and as such, have tackled roles from Tulsa to Conrad Birdie to Captain Hook and coveted roles from Reno Sweeney to Mame to both Maria's - *West Side* as well as *The Sound of Mucus* (not a typo).

Kyle wears his signature big, sparkly belt buckle. He has his ear pierced and has the most infectious smile this side of the Cheshire Cat. He lives with Robert, a suave young Latino, several years his junior with excessive hair product, in a little house on the East side of town. They have a cat, Judy Garland, and they throw incredible parties. I've never in my life known two men who *lived together* and I'm intrigued; perhaps even envious. I am sixteen and he is thirty-something, and we're great friends. I like Kyle.

At the Saturday matinee of *You're a Good Man Charlie Brown,* during the scene in the show when Peppermint Patty reads her book report aloud to Ms. Othmar (the teacher with the slide trombone accent), Peppermint Patty can't stop laughing. She's turning red in front of the audience and cannot get through the song. On the inside of her book report, a prop consisting of multi colored pieces of construction paper, Kyle (who plays Schroeder) has pasted cut outs from a magazine -- *Blue Boy.* Totally nude, buff, adonis-like men sun themselves in exotic locals and there's a centerfold with a safari theme. This particular prop mysteriously disappears from the set shortly thereafter and somehow makes it into my book bag.

My friend Kyle. Who, when I was asked (after a phenomenal audition, by the way) to merely run props for *The King and I*, demanded that I be given the title "Property Master" in the program, a title we both learned one day while watching the closing credits of *The Golden Girls*. And he also negotiates that I will make a brief cameo as a *Siamese priest*.

Robert split following the first bought with pneumonia and that was the last any of us ever heard from him until we saw his wedding announcement in the newspaper not long thereafter. "Well, hon" as Kyle said, "I suppose that leaves me with a very important distinction - I have officially *scared* a man *straight!"*

It's his twilight days and we're hanging out at his house, where he's been confined for months, our little local hospital unable and unwilling to care for him. "Hey hon - you wanna hear some music? Here - I'll put on *South Pacific,* that always makes you smile, you're such a sap that way. Oh, do stop frowning. *Forget your troubles, come on, get happy!*" He moves so slowly about the apartment now, which seems so empty without Robert. I pretend not to notice.

"Would you take this for me? I just can't bear the thought of my sister finding it and throwing it out."

And he hands me the flashy gold belt buckle that we'd all come to associate with Kyle. The bright, shiny piece of gold metal that he always wore with such flare and that says so much about the man who dares to don it. "Just hold onto it for me for awhile, hm, hon?"

And I leave Kyle's house that day with not only his fabulous belt buckle, but also with Judy Garland. "Ok, mister cat - you take care of my friend here, ok? I'll see ya real soon. ... *Goodbye.*"

The very first funeral I ever attended in my life was Kyle's, and I *so wish* that I could say that it was my last. We're all there that day, dressed in black. I have never known anybody who died. Kyle comes from a large Indiana family but none of them are present that day, none of his blood family. And not two hours later, we're all in the dressing room getting made up for that evening's performance of *Annie*. There's an erriee silence in the room, eyes all downcast as we apply makeup, -- there is a profound absence. How will we possibly go out and sing about our hard knock lives and the sun coming up tomorrow when Kyle and his infectious smile are nowhere to be found?

But when I go out on stage that night - I see him. It sounds romantic, but I actually *see him*. He's running around the orchestra pit and mooning Miss Hannigan, - a part I know he covets. He's making fun of the orphans and holding up signs telling us where we're hanging out for wine and mozzarella sticks after the show. He's smiling up at us, just beaming... at home in the solace that we both found in the theatre.

And in so many many ways, - he's here right now.

BESSIE

My little blue Honda is my pride and joy. It was love at first site when I saw her at the Honda dealer on South Taylor Road, sitting on the lot, neglected in a corner with the cars headed for the scarp yard. My parental units, eager to be free of their chauffer responsibilities, are only too happy to fork over the two thousand dollars out right. I am handed keys -- *and I am free!*

My vehicle will need a name, of course, so that it knows it's wanted and cared for - *Bessie.* Yes, Bessie the little blue Honda, named for Bessie Smith. Bessie and I have a special relationship - she takes me places. I adorn her backseat with throw pillows and a macramé shawl and accessorize the floorboards with small mats that resemble rugs from the orient. Bessie takes me to ordinary places like the movies and pizza parlors on evenings when my mother and stepfather declare "date night," and I am hence banished from the house and asked not to return till well past nightfall. But on bright Spring days she also takes me speeding through cornfields at ninety miles an hour - so fast that the car actually shakes, as I belt Bette Midler's *The Rose* at the top of my lungs with the windows down and the sunroof open. She takes me to the theatre in Indianapolis, to concerts in Louisville, and of course to all of the myriad cultural offerings available in Columbus, Indiana. Bessie is my escape pod, my traveling companion, my friend. We are deeply committed to each other.

It's happened more than once. Bessie is injured and I mourn. Exiting the school auditorium, where I have been deep in rehearsal for our show choir presentation of *Broadway!* (exclamation point!), the reflection of glass greets me before I see it - Bessie's headlights - her eyes - have been smashed in, laying about in shards upon the parking lot pavement. And this would happen over and over again, along with the occasional tire slash. Bessie has been tagged - a target. And if Bessie is a target - then so must I be.

My mother and stepfather have left town, and this is ecstasy. How I amuse myself making believe the house is not only my own but really a grand mansion to which I have invited the crown heads of Europe for supper and dancing, after which we are to be entertained by Streisand and LuPone. I take pride in making my own dinner, setting the table with the good silver, lighting candles, playing my own music, being self-reliant. I sleep soundly through the night with my dog, Nicky Arnstein, listening to the house creak and dreaming of all the things I know I'll one day be.

In the morning, having donned the proper wardrobe for another endlessly boring day at school, I make my way out to the drive to find my friend Bessie decimated. She is a shell of her former self. Not just her eyes are broken this time but her face - the windshield, is shattered - all of the windows are smashed through, the sunroof is gone, taken as a souvenir, I suppose. All the tires are slashed, the hood and doors have been beaten with a bat and words like "Faggot" and "Homo" writ large with - what appears to be toothpaste. Dog feces has been left in the driver's seat. My bedroom, located in the back of the house, has prevented me from hearing this, but the neighbors - surely the neighbors must have noticed or heard. ... And I realize, yes - *yes,* they probably did. Windows surround me, and looking to each of them, it seems that I am on stage, not one of my own choosing this time, and a performance of sorts has commenced.

Well, that ought to teach me. I will cripple their ruthless act of aggression with defiance. In time I will forgive them for not knowing any better. In time I will try to forget that they took my friend, my little blue Honda, Bessie, my *freedom* from me. In time I will wonder if they ever think about this or if they have banished it from their minds just as I never will. I will wonder if they remain proud of their actions, laughing about it still over nights at red neck bars in wherever they ended up. But for now, I strap on my Walkman, armed with a cassette - *Merrily We Roll Along,* and I walk to school.

OLD, SILLY, BALD MEN

He is old and fat and silly, and he wants me to come back to his hotel room with him.

"Auh… I think I have to meet up with my

group," is what I say, even though I think he's funny and he fascinates sixteen-year-old me.

"Whatever for? *Heavens…*" is his grand response. His pale brow furrows amongst the wrinkles. His eyes, smaller because they are encased by fat, look as though they are trying to see behind my corneas and directly into my brain, an X-ray technique I sense him using when he looks other places, as well.

I am flattered. Truly, I am. Nobody has ever looked at me like that before. Even if he is old and wrinkled and bald, he makes me feel somehow important. He takes me to dinner along with the really important people from the theatre conference, all the board members and the high-end donors. I let him buy me a steak and compliment me in front of everyone all night long. Wow. This could really be a jumping off point for me. If I can impress the folks from the League of Indiana

Community Theatres, there's *no telling* what might happen.

I'm feeling more than a bit adventuresome in my new, sharp-looking dinner clothes. It all feels so adult: culinary schmoozing in hotel restaurants. He insists that I eat the seaweed ice cream, which he loves and I find beyond vile: "It cleanses the palate..." his hand reaches for my knee under the table. "It's so so marvelous to see you. And looking so, so well." He's the first man I've ever met who uses the word 'marvelous' in an ordinary sentence. He certainly won't be the last. Thank God.

He has large pieces of purple and pink plastic strewn around his neck on a string, which he wears as a necklace. He is wearing a sports coat with a navy sweatshirt underneath, and brown corduroy trousers, which don't quite stretch all the way around his waist.

"Thank you for dinner," I smile broadly and

take my leave. He follows me out of the dining room and to the elevator. I cannot refuse him, he is from NEW YORK!! So many years, when I have stood at the bus stop on those frigid school mornings, waiting to be shipped off to another day of misery, watching my breath hang in the air in front of me, preparing for hours of useless Algebra and Biology and Trigonometry - I look to the East, over the rooftops of suburbia, and I imagine I can see the lights of the Great White Way.

"Come back to my room with me. I have to get something," he implores, guiding me toward a different elevator. I am afraid, if not a little bit amused, even curious. I know what he has to get. Still, to be close to someone, to have someone touch me, would be nice. I actually consider it for a split second, the security that comes with the intimate presence of another body, however old and wrinkled and bald. To feel so young and so beautiful, to feel so desired is an intoxication all its own.

"I don't think that's a good idea," I say, and he never speaks to me again. And this is sad. Soon, he goes home to New York, that golden land of which I dream, and I go home to the corn, but not before he hugs me goodbye for far, far too long.

However, I know he senses my midwestern boredom, having once been, perhaps, a fabulous child trapped in corn county himself, and therefore I begin receiving packages in the mail from New York: Playbills, postcards, a miniature statue of Michelangelo's David, exciting trinkets from the artistic hub of the universe. And I never get the opportunity to adequetly thank him.

When I move to New York years from now, I will see Eddie at the theatre every now and then. He will refuse to speak to me even still, but rather glance over at me from across the aisle, and wink.

Old, silly, bald men: grand dames of the theatre. I'd live to know a million of them. They make me feel pretty, - for now. But to quote Sam Cooke: *"change gonna come..."*

EYEBROWS

Billie Holiday soothes my broken seventeen-year-old heart. I am fortunate to have stumbled across her music so early in life, hence beginning a life of the blues all the sooner. She wails, *and I pluck.*

I decided about a year before that my eyebrows as they were would never do. They form a natural point at the top of the arch, which causes me to bare a remarkable resemblance to Margaret Hamilton in *The Wizard of Oz*. They are much too close together. A uni-brow is simply not becoming on someone of my coloring. Hence, since the time I am fifteen, I pluck and configure my brows into what I consider to be a more appealing form.

Oh, Christ... *sing it,* Billie. Michael has left me. My first boyfriend is gone. And when your man is gone, *your world just falls apart*, according to Barbra. I am a straw in the wind.

I have been dumped. It is the kind of breakup that has left me sick to my stomach, in a constant state of uneasiness and frailty. I recall my favorite scene from *The Helen Keller Story*: "Who will ever love *me,* mama? Where is the love for *me,* mama?" I have stopped eating, under the bizarre subconscious assumption that if I starve myself long enough, he will at least insist on having dinner with me. It's all so pathetic, a fact that even I realize my seventeen-year-old eyes are too young to see. But this does not comfort a heart first broken. Besides, I am enjoying playing Katie in *The Way We Were* far too much.

Michael is a beautiful dancer from the other

high school across town, and I have allowed myself to fall for him tights over dance belt. He has led me to believe that the feeling is mutual all during our two-week relationship, a courtship comprised of shared meals at Steak and Shake and lots of bad kissing.

Love is very young in us both, and everything fresh and unexpected, like a new toy. We have really nothing in common and we basically bore each other, but no matter. We're two queer kids amongst the Indiana corn. Besides, it is the act itself, the idea of being together in and of itself that is so thrilling, enough to put smiles on both of our faces, at least for the time being.

But he has left me for another man: *a soccer player.* Betrayed at seventeen, a woman scorned: *I am Hedda Gabler.* Michael is gone now. I am alone in the woods yet again.

Billie Holiday drones on. Later, I will head to

Blockbuster to rent *The Way We Were* or maybe *Love Story*, too. Perhaps, just like Barbra in the movie, he will see me on the street years from now, wearing a tan raincoat and looking dashing and beautiful, and he will run his fingers through my hair and remark how I am no longer ironing it. And perhaps he will invite me to dinner and, unlike the film, perhaps I will accept. Perhaps someday we will be together again. And I cling to this. Please, God... *let him come back.*

I am alone in the house and I play the torch songs as loudly as the speakers can stand it. I cannot sing along, *for I am too weak.* It is too much effort to exert. I am too weak to dress, even, and so I roam the house in my robe. I am abandoned, neglected, wounded. ... *And so I pluck.*

This is the first time that my heart has broken, and I secretly rejoice in the pain, because it means that I actually have one. I have no way of knowing that this is merely the beginning. The world spins upon an axis of heartbreak, and yet it continues to spin just the same. And people continue to laugh all over the world. Perhaps I will learn. Someday. But for the moment, *I pluck.*

Suddenly I stop. Gazing at my pained and tear-streaked face in the bathroom mirror for a long moment, I realize… *a bit too much. … A lot* too much. Bit by bit, little by little, and torch song after torch song, I have lost my conscious self in pity and ignored the fact that I now bare a striking resemblance to Whoopi Goldberg, my brows plucked to mere faint lines atop my eyes.

Embarrassed and nervous, I run to my mother's bedroom to swipe one of her eyebrow pencils. I delicately fill in my brows, praying I will someday be able to once again show my mutilated self in public.

My mother and stepfather arrive home from

the grocery store (they like to shop *as a couple.* Cute.) and I mope into the kitchen, head to the floor. What does it matter if they notice, anyway? My entire existence lay shattered on the soiled floor of false dreams.

"Did you pluck your eyebrows?" His is a voice of disgust that goes unmasked. He has never liked me and never will.

"Don't be doing that!' She jumps in, taking a respite from shoving the Holly Farm chicken into the freezer (the same kind Dinah Shore eats!) She is dodging a larger conversation that she is not yet ready to have with her son, and so for the moment, all she can utter is "I don't want you *doing* that!" She glares at me with her enflamed eyes, enlarged with rage, embarrassed for her new husband to see the wires that hold up our lives. I secretly pray that soon they will both catch me kissing some man, or better.

"That's downright queer," is all he says, and I wonder if he will raise a hand this time. Instead, he offers a look of disgust, and walks into the living room to seek better company with my dog, Nicky Arnstein - who routinely growls at him until swatted, whereupon he skulks out of the room upon his furry paws, in search of me.

As I watch my stepfather leave the room, this bully, this man who replaces joy with fear, who has forced me to develop body armor of my own design at a very early age, I can't help but wonder: *what happened to him?* What evil elements conspired to mold this man? Did he ever have a fighting chance at being kind? And for a fleeting moment, I find sympathy. But it vanishes very very quickly.

We never discuss eyebrows again.

PINE IN A BOTTLE

The house is covered in pine: down the banister, around the furniture and hanging from the doorknobs along with the little jingle bells that sound like a blaring alarm every time somebody opens the door. A bottle of liquid scent has even been procured, "Pine in a Bottle," which has been sprayed all about the house. Christmas is here, *like it or not,* and the family has gathered near.

I've returned from college this year, for this festive season, for what would be my last Christmas at home, and I think I may just throw up pine-scented vomit. The only thing that saves us during the holidays is the family tradition that gatherings such as these should be accompanied by copious amounts of alcohol.

I sit alone by the fire as my family amuse themselves watching silly sports games on television. It's Christmas Eve, and what could say "holiday" more than the Colts verses the Knicks?

Thank the Baby Jesus, my stepfather has this momentous event on *videotape.*

"This game was one for the history books!" he declares in all of his ignorant, sweatshirt-wearing bravado.

I sing Carpenters Christmas songs in my head and try to conjure images of that Maxwell House commercial, the one where the cute blonde gay kid comes home on Christmas morning and his sister wakes up and then the whole family?

The doorbell rings. In walks Dennis. *Hello, Dennis*: my boyfriend before I shipped off for college, still alone in the woods and the corn of Indiana, eagerly awaiting my return. Oh, there is happiness. A caller from my homeland, it seems, has come to join the festivities: a gift from the Magi. I smile for the first time that December.

My stepbrothers aren't so much shocked, but more fascinated, as he presents my mother with a gift, a beeswax candle, and joins us all in the living room without hesitation, sitting down next to me by the fire. All eyes are upon us as my stepfather mixes Dennis a Manhattan and refills mine. I pray that my stepfather will spare us the demonstration of how he can tie a cherry stem into a knot using only his tongue. We hadn't expected Dennis, but *this could get fun.*

My mother and stepfather sit entwined on the sofa, my stepbrother and his wife do the same over by the window, my other stepbrother and his girlfriend are nearly to the point of conception over by the sliding glass door. Once there's enough alcohol coursing through everyone's blood, Dennis puts his arm around me in front of the fire, and I simply relax into it.

Christmas Eve is terribly romantic; this is the first year I've realized it. Someone who wants to put their arm around me by a fireplace, even if accompanied by the sounds of a sports broadcaster, is joyful. For a moment, I think that perhaps they see that, too. And for the first Christmas since my early youth, I realize how perfect it is to be surrounded by loved ones. I'm seeing Christmas in a whole different light.

Soon everyone has gone to bed. The house is dark, and Dennis and I trample off to my bedroom. The same room where I have spent so much time alone, where I once dreamed of Barbra and Carol and nursed broken hearts, cried over mutilated eyebrows and cursed the world, now houses me and this beautiful naked man who dared to love me in front of other people.

Being with Dennis in my boyhood home is exciting, if not somehow ironic. It seems somehow wrong, but then, so miraculously right. It's quiet. Warmth surrounded by the cold walls of my youth. The male body is a stunning work of art, so perfectly formed and amazing to touch. How I wish we could wake up together on Christmas morning and he would kiss me hello. But of course, I know this is not possible. He will soon venture out to his snow-covered Ford Escort and drive away into the night, hoping that the sound of his engine starting does not wake my slumbering mother and stepfather. In the morning, in the light of the day, everything will change. And once this visit to my homeland comes to an end, I will never see this house nor this place again.

Still, for the moment, embraced by his bare arms and resting beside his warm body, amidst the trophies and ribbons that represent my boyhood triumphs, it all feels so grown up. I've learned to kiss and do other things, as well, including some unique tongue tricks of my own. Wouldn't my stepfather be impressed?

THE BIRTH

He can't seem to get the eyes right. He drags the brush across my eyelid, extending the line way out onto my face, but it's just not quite right yet, despite Fernando's exuberant compliments of his own work.

"You look *fierce!*" he proclaims. I have waited pensively to make my drag debut. I have always said that if I were going to do it, I would do it right: get a professional to make me over with the gown, the wig, the makeup, rather than entrust my clumsy self with Max Factor and heels. So, as a college graduation present, my friend Fernando agrees to give me the works.

The gown is gorgeous: beaded sequins with a long slit up the leg, reaching almost to my hipbone. I wear the four inch heels all day, trying to break them in and get used to the feel of being six foot nine. People in the office look at me oddly, especially during the early morning staff meeting as I cross and uncross my legs. Standing at the copier, I realize what a long way down to the start button it is, true on so many levels.

He's finished the eyes, finally. Only a little more rogue on the cheekbones and some powder, and the picture is complete. My cleavage is a construction of pantyhose packaging and makeup, adequate to trick the eye *from a distance*. The wig and fire red lipstick are both in place now, and he is lacing up the same high heels in which I have practiced all day so diligently. The final thing is the cape, a long, flowing piece of fabric with zebra print on the inside that matches my long, elbow-length gloves. A final dab of powder and a touch-up of mascara, and the creation is finished.

Standing, I turn to look at myself in the mirror. I have left my body and become someone else. It is a completely altered me who looks back at me in the reflection, my former self is hidden in a menagerie of color and lacquer. Jesus Christ, I look like my mother. Wig and shoes combined, I am nearly seven feet tall. Wouldn't this make my stepfather happy, I think: I can finally play basketball.

My legs, wrapped in fishnet stockings, are long and striking. He has made my eyes large and beautiful and accentuated my bone structure … I'm pretty.

I do not walk, but rather *descend* the stairs that lead into the ball, which for tonight has taken the form of a Latin dance club in the west thirties of bustling New York City. As I make my way down, I recall the stone steps in the backyard of my big white mansion and those fantastic black patent leather, Princess Leia boots. I can hear Barbra in my ear.

I will most likely never do this again in my

life; it's really quite uncomfortable. But for tonight, for now, it's new and it's glamorous; and I love it.

All eyes are on me as I strut my way through the club, saturated in dry ice, holding my own on the dance floor filled with hunky Latino boys, a few of whom ask me to feel the sweat upon their masculine torsos with my long, painted red fingernails. "You look hot, Mommie!" a shirtless Adonis cries out. And I do.

I emerge from the ladies room, which I use without batting a false eyelash, when suddenly I see him. Turning on my stiletto I see him right there, over by the bar and huddled in a corner. It's that abandoned thirteen year old boy from the woods - it's *me,* or the ghost of me; alone on a singular summer afternoon beneath a sky scratched with cloud - shrouded amongst the silence of the trees that sway in the wind, left alone and wondering *what* he did wrong. And I reach out to him with my bejeweled hand and I stroke the side of his scared face. And I say to him - you frightened little boy in the woods, -- *I will find you.* It doesn't seem like it now, but *I will find you...* And if you're wondering if there's a second act to all of this ... KID, *you better believe it.* Now then, in the words of Joan Crawford via Faye Dunaway, the greatest spectacle of casting ever created: *...Let's go.*

The music hits a climax and there is a flash of white light. For the first time in my life, I have the right moves and I execute them to the beat of the music.

Muffin Coffee is awake.

PHIL GEOFFREY BOND is an award-winning author, best known for his collection of short pieces, *All the Sad Young Men,* and the celebrated picture book, *My Friend, the Cat,* based on the popular stage show. Often mixing dramatic prose with live theatre, his original pieces *My Queer Youth, The Disney Diaries, My Friend, the Cat, My Roaring Twenties* and *Small Town Confessions* have been embraced by a wide range of off-Broadway audiences. As a playwright, Phil has developed work at The Sundance Theatre Lab *(The Citadel),* and at many regional theatres throughout the states. A fixture on the NYC nightlife scene, he is a seven-time MAC (Manhattan Association of Cabarets), two-time Bistro and one-time Nightlife Award-winner. Currently, he is the writer/producer/host of *Sondheim Unplugged,* now enjoying it's sixth year at Manhattan nightspot Feinstein's/54 Below, where he also created the popular *54 Sings* series and served as the venue's first Director of Programming and later Director of Original Programming. 2016 will see the release of his debut novel, *The Last Year at Low Tide* (Chess Books). In 1993, he was awarded the Presidential Medallion from President Clinton on behalf of his work as a young playwright. www.philgeoffreybond.com.

Also by Phil Geoffrey Bond

My Friend, the Cat
2006, Chess Books

My Friend, the Cat traces the humorous and touching ten year relationship, complete with pictures, between a young man and one very adventuresome feline, Chesterson. From chasing cockroaches in their first apartment, "a crappy East Village monstrosity with sloping floors," where, during hot summers, kitty was placed in the refrigerator to cool off, to wintertime road trips where we learn that cats can indeed drive a station wagon, straight through to the furry one's cold-blooded attacks upon sleeping bare feet, the story of this special union unfolds year by year.

All the Sad Young Men
2009, Chess Books

All the Sad Young Men is the debut collection of short works from Phil Geoffrey Bond. Part fiction, part autobiographical, the locales span the bright lights of a twisted urban jungle to the sunny cornfields of southern Indiana. From Disney World to Greenwich Village, felines to Fire Island, super models to stuffed bears, *All the Sad Young Men* is a varied and provocative literary work from a new American voice.

The Disney Diaries
2016, Chess Books

What happens when a wayward homosexual from New York City heads down to Orlando for the annual "Gay Days" celebration, culminating with a "magical" day at The Magic Kingdom? From the flying elephants of Fantasyland to the raging waters of Splash Mountain, hilarity (and a touch of cynicism) ensues as 135,000 red shirted gays descend upon the happiest place on Earth.

Small Town Confessions
2016, Chess Books

Applebee's. Aliens. Jesus Christ. Disney Princesses. Show choir. Glittery nail polish: The folks down in Anitola Parish got it all. Drop by! It's more fun than church and better than a night at the Wal-Mart! *Small Town Confessions* concerns the "special" residents of Anitola Parish, Louisiana. Rumors of visits from martians, a special stopover from Diana Ross, an obsession with the musical *Wicked,* a has-been Walt Disney World employee, a chat with the bride of Satan and the creative use of spray glitter are all tales told in this homespun account of small town living. The proceedings are hosted by Jobeth Maybelline, manicurist to the town and keeper of community secrets.

www.ingramcontent.com/pod-product-compliance
Lightning Source LLC
Chambersburg PA
CBHW020559030426
42337CB00013B/1149